TRUTH AND GREATNESS

TRUTH AND GREATNESS

MICHAEL "TRUTH" GRAHAM
STEFFANI JEMISON
KHOREY "GREATNESS" SMITH

TABLE OF CONTENTS

7

73

93

Truth and Greatness: A Nonfiction Novella *Steffani Jemison*

Invisible Ink: Third-Person Autobiography
Michael Graham and Khorey Smith

A Glass Half-Empty *Michael Graham and Khorey Smith*

Truth lies on the carpet; papers and pencils are spread out before him on the floor. Greatness walks in."So, we got any ideas?" Greatness asks, as he begins to fiddle with the computer.

"No," Truth laughs. "Hell naw. I mean," he continues, scratching his head, "I got the other idea I told you in the car."

"You mean about how we can put all the lines together?"

"Yeah." He begins to spread pieces of paper in a row in front of him.

"I'd say right now, we should read through 'em. So we can get a feel for it."

"Alright."

"Start on..."

"... three years ago."

"So the first page is basically like, 'Three years ago and before the twins were born...' 'Even after all she had been through during her crack addiction, Laci was still fly.' 'You gave it to 'em sis! You did your thang, girl.' 'Life in Houston was a bit different.' 'Now I'm sitting here all alone, in my hair shop, thinking about what I'm going to do about this baby I'm carrying.'"

"I don't know how we're going to do that."

"'Why you so worried about it? I got this.'"

"There's a baby in the story."

"And there's a mother in the story, obviously."

"True."

"'... straighten things up around my two-bedroom, two-bath condo until my telephone started ringing.'"

"'See what God can do, if you believe? You will achieve.' 'My face was innocent, but that was about it.' I like that line." He says it again. "'My face was innocent. But that was about it.'"

Greatness laughs. "'I told you God had our backs, didn't I?' It's funny how people say that, but they don't know who God really is."

Truth interjects, "According to Greatness."

Greatness, raising his eyebrows, "Yeah, yeah. Quote me on that."

Truth laughs. "Bitch."

"Shut up."

"Uh, let's see."

"'But after a lot of late night grinding, stacking, and going without while they all partied and kicked it, I soon escalated above him.' Now where exactly are they going with that? Cause that's like an Edgar Allen Poe line to me."

"I don't know."

"I mean, it's totally random, like something I would say."

"Cause you do be saying random stuff."

"Shut up."

"You shut up."

"'I'm dying! She screamed so loud her neighbors could hear. She never looked back, running as fast as her wobbly legs would carry her. She never even took a breath.'"

"Keep running, even if that means you're still going to lose." Truth's tone is mocking.

"Shut up!" Now Greatness is insulted. Truth is attacking not only his favorite poem, but also his romantic failures.

"All the way till the end!"

"Hell yeah. You can't—" Greatness gropes for an insult "—you can't write a love piece for nothing."

"I don't care."

"Shut up."

Truth went back to his notes. "'... started living each day as if it were my last.' 'I don't want you to come tomorrow.' 'Can you be a soldier, help out a general...'" he mumbles.

"That's like a colorful metaphor."

"Yeah. 'Same shit, different day!' Greatness, we back here, the same shit, different day." Greatness claps.

"'I know I'm getting ready to make a move, and when I do, I got you.' That sound like some hood stuff for real. Like something somebody in the hood say when they getting ready to jump somebody."

"You already know we can't do that whole 'hood' thing." Truth makes scare quotes with his fingers.

"Yeah. I mean, the thing is to be universal."

"Course. Cause you know they expecting that. Black people do black stuff, apparently."

"Enough on your people," Greatness tells Truth, then continues, reading. "'I'm going to be ugly today and I'm going to be ugly tomorrow.'"

"You're ugly now. How does that sound?"

"Shut up! Yo mama's ugly now."

"Bitch, yo mama is fine."

Greatness laughs. "My mama is. And I came out according to plan. You, I don't know." He looks back at the paper. "'And if you still wanna come by, I still wanna see you.' That sound like something your whipped ass would say."

Truth smiles. "Course." Then, "Excuse me, wait, what?"

"Yee-uh."

"I ain't whipped."

"*Whipped.*"

"Shut up."

"Taking Queen to the Beyoncé concert. That's whipped!"

"When's the last time you took your girlfriend?"

"Shut up."

Truth laughs. "Oh wait," he says, joking. "'There's no use in me dwellin' on shit I can't change.' That's some shit that you would say."

"Shut up. Negative."

"You're negative."

"'Coming from nothing and having nothing are two different things," Greatness reads. "Yeah, I came from nothing, but I was determined to have it all. How couldn't I?'"

"I don't understand 'how couldn't I.'"

"Who—who wrote that?"

"I don't understand the 'how couldn't I' part. 'How couldn't I?'"

"'They say a cat has nine lives. Although many describe me as having feline characteristics, the skill of escaping death seemed to be what we shared most in common.' 'Please let him still be available.'"

"'Shit's for the birds, baby. I'm ready to go.'"

"What does that mean?" Greatness snorts. "'Game over, I don't feel like playing anymore.' 'I didn't get an answer.' 'Many say a dream is a premonition of what the future holds, but as I fought the demons in my nightmare, I prayed that not to be the truth.' This is very ... *that*'s a punch line. We can—we should come up with ways to..."

"'The time has finally come for the verdict.' 'I'm tired of hearing this same ole story.'"

"'If school was ever in session with you, maybe I could learn a thing or two from you. But it seems that you're always out to lunch.'"

"Speaking of which, I'm hungry."

"Now that line is dope. That line is dope. That's kinda like that super smart student that when you try to learn something from them they never want to help you."

"They can't teach your ass, that's why. They're like, I don't know how this is explained and you're like," he smacks his lips, "you just got a fucking 99."

"On the damn test."

"On the damn test and you're telling me you can't explain it."

"'From this day forward she was feeding herself daily. She reveled in her newfound independence.' 'There's absolutely nothing slow about me but the way I walk.'"

Truth takes off his tie. "You tell 'em."

Greatness says, "I'll let you tell it."

"You're just slow."

"'And despite my hardships I held my head high. I'd learned that bad things happened to good people. My life was bad. My heart was good.' Yes. That would make for a critical explanation."

"There we go. We got a nigga phrase."

"Oh. Nigga moment."

"Nigga moment. 'We don't need another nigga eatin' off our plate.'"

"Sound like something somebody would say."

"No 'n' words! We have to fix that."

"'Just do the damn thing.' 'Nard hit him with the strike of magic and poof, just like that, Jeremy was gone.' Who is Jeremy?"

Truth laughs. "Who is Nard?"

"I don't know."

"'Sometimes a woman had to kill herself to survive.'"

"*What?*"

"That could be some deep stuff, you know what I'm saying? We could flip that."

"That would be you saying that, with your suicidal ass."

"Shut up. Shut up."

"'My mother hated me, my father disowned me, stepfather molested me, Johns used me, ex-husband abused me.' She has a pretty messed up life."

"Johns used me. Johns..."

"Who is Johns?"

"Johns. You know, we could—I got an idea for how we could use that."

"What?"

"Like the Bible. The book of Johns." Greatness drops his head to his hands. "I'm so serious."

"The Bible?"

"The Bible. That would be a dope moment."

"Be careful, cause—"

"—we'll figure out this line—"

"—no quoting from the Bible..."

"Yes, yes, I know, I know."

"It's blasphemy."

"I know. But we'll figure it out."

"'God, you gave me a brain, courage, and a heart. Tell me which one to use before I kill both of these fools.' Now that sounds like something I say." Truth nods in agreement. "That was the appropriate place for this particular line," Greatness says, underlining with a pen. "'Hopefully my day will come very soon,' that sounds like—"

"What are you talking about?"

"I mean it's like one of the last sentences on the page. So, I mean maybe..."

"She just put the lines on the page!"

"I know she put the lines on the page, but let's not be ignorant about this."

"Okay, so you're saying there's an order for a reason."

"I mean, not necessarily an order for a reason, but it might have been a coincidence."

"You and your coincidences. Whatever."

"Shut up."

"Alright, so. Okay okay okay, check this out, check this out. Because what we could do is—I don't know about you but I saw a whole bunch of different types of lines in here that we could probably label."

"Yeah, I was thinking kind of like the same thing."

"Okay, like check this out. The 'three years and before the twins were born, 'that's an introduction line."

"An introduction line..."

"So what we need to—"

"We'll just put a star by that one."

"Okay. Well then, let's find all the introduction lines and you said put a star by them?"

"Yeah."

"I like to put a highlight or something..." Truth pulls out a green highlighter.

"Yeah." Greatness holds a blue highlighter. "Start by 'Three years ago.'"

"What else is an introduction line?"

"'Even after all she had been through...'"

"That's not an introduction line."

"Basically, an introductory line is a line that's not quoted."

"Okay."

"Here we go. 'Before I go any further allow me to introduce myself.'"

"What page is that?"

"Second."

"'... trying to live each day as if it were my last... There's all different types of lines in here, so it's best if we uh..." Truth points to something on his page and Greatness highlights something on his own paper. They exchange glances. "This is an introductory line?"

"Sure."

"I thought this was a punch line. Either a punch line or a description line."

"No, let's just do an introductory. Okay, wait."

"You sure?"

"Yeah. Let's just put a star by it. Okay so what do we usually do? Why don't we just do what we usually do. We'll go over what type of lines we have, and then we'll just kind of, I guess wing it from there. We got introductory lines, we'll put a star by those. What other type of lines we have?"

"I see some interracial lines by here. Like, I'm dying."

"I got you. So we got interracial lines. What are we going to put for those?"

"We'll just put brackets."

"Brackets for interracial lines?"

"Like so. Like that."

"Which one did you do?"

"'I'm dying, she screams so loud her neighbors can hear.' You know, they got a quote, and then they got a descriptive line in it."

"Okay what other lines?"

"Okay yeah, I found another one. On the same page. 'I started living each day as if it were my last.' 'One more motherfucking time, he whispered.' 'I'm getting ready to make a move' … naw, that's not it. Not necessarily. Not yet."

"I know there's more. What other type of lines?"

"We got some narrative lines. Like the lines that tell a story. Like 'we used to be so happy' or 'we had it all.'"

"What are we going to put for narratives?"

"For narratives we'll put a check by it."

"Check baby, check baby, one two three. Check baby, check baby, one two."

"Quit playing."

"Shut up."

"'I started living each day as if it were my last.' Is that a narrative line?"

"Yeah."

"'Can you be a soldier and help out a general.' Sound like something Lil Wayne would say. Kind of like a metaphor or…"

"That's a punch line."

"Yeah. So what are we going to put for that?"

"Let's put 'p.' 'Soon she would have to find him.'"

"'She would certainly have to find him.'"

"That sounds like a narrative line."

"Check it."

"'There was no way she could live there. The world goes so fast, too fast.' Sounds like another narrative line."

"'That dream, it's starting again. That same dream.' Um. That's a descriptive line."

"No."

"No, it's not descriptive because it doesn't say anything. It doesn't tell me anything."

"I know one thing we can do. Remember I was telling you in the car that we could chop and screw some of these."

"Mmm hmm."

"Yeah we can do that."

"Is that line one of them?"

"Yeah, because think about it if you said that dream, it's starting again, that same dream. You know what I'm saying? So put a 'c.'"

"'I told you I'm not going anywhere.' Now what's that? That's a narrative line, right?

"Naw, that's a chop it up line. Chop it up, chop it up, chop it up."

"'... they got back to what they were doing before I walked up.' That is a narrative line."

"Check it. 'Same shit, different day.'"

"That's a punch. Naw, it's not a punch line."

"That's narrative, dude."

"Narrative?"

"Cliché."

"I don't know about all that. 'But when I do I got you.' There should be something for slang phrases."

"Okay. Well then put 'S-L' for slang. 'Same shit, different day' is slang."

"'Seems like the shoe is on the other foot now.'" Greatness coughs.

"That's narrative?"

"No. Hardly. I'd say it's a slang."

"What the hell?"

"It's a mixture between slang and narrative. You could use it for either one. Put both. 'I'm ready to get my own.'"

"That could be used as slang or narrative."

"Narrative. This is descriptive. Descriptive, descriptive, descriptive. What are we doing with descriptive?"

"Underline ... underscore."

"'If you still want to come by, I still want to see you.' That could be a punch line."

"Yeah."

"I got some shit for that. Seriously."

"'Even after all she had did' ... that's a descriptive line. 'You gave it to 'em sis. You did yo thang, girl.'"

"Slang."

"'God is good.'"

"You could state that as an extreme phrase or extreme quote."

"Religious phrase?"

"Or we could do it like that. Religious. Just put 'R.' 'It's a sign, I know it.' That's a chop line." Greatness looks up at Truth for affirmation.

"Okay, chop line."

"'Life in Houston was a bit different.' That's narrative. 'Now I'm sitting'... descriptive."

"'What you so worried about? I got this.'"

"Slang. 'Afterward I began to straighten things up around my two bedroom'... descriptive. 'And now the moment you've been waiting for.'"

"Introductory."

"'See look what God can do. If you believe, you can achieve.'"

"Religious." Greatness can't stop coughing, and stands up to get a glass of water.

"What the hell's wrong with you?"

"I don't know." He sits back down. "'... blessed like this.' Religious. 'Her face was innocent but that was about it.' Punch line."

"Punch line."

"'I told you God had our backs, didn't I?' Religious. 'But after a lot of late night'... that's a narrative line."

"That's descriptive."

"What is it describing? Okay."

"'She never looked back, running as fast as her wobbly legs would carry her. She never even took a breath.' That is a..."

"Descriptive."

"Yeah. Descriptive. 'There's no use in me dwelling on shit I can't change. That is...'"

"Narrative."

"Yeah, I suppose. It can be used as a narrative or a punch line in some context. It would be good if we could find out where all these lines gotta be used. 'Being from nothing and coming from nothing are two different things.' Okay, that is a narrative line. 'They say a cat has nine lives.' That's a punch line."

"It's a long-ass punch line."

"Mmm-hmm."

"'Please let him still be available.' 'This shit is for the birds'... slang. 'Game over, I don't feel like playing anymore.'"

"That's a punch line."

"Alright. 'I ain't getting mad, son.' It could be used as a punch line in the right context. That's a narrative line. 'I'm tired of the same old story.'"

"Yeah?"

"Yeah. 'If school was ever in session with you, maybe I could learn a thing or two from you, but it seems that you're always out to lunch.' That's a punch line. That's a punch line something serious. 'From this day forward she was feeding herself daily. She reveled in her newfound independence.' That's not a punch line."

Truth's drumming his hands. Greatness's eyes look almost closed. "Descriptive?" Truth suggests.

"Mmm-hmm. 'There's absolutely nothing slow about me but the way I walk.'"

"Oh no, you're just slow period."

"That's a punch line. 'Despite my hardships I held my head high...'"

"Descriptive."

"Slang."

"That's a nigger line."

"We are not gonna write down that, 'nigger line.' 'We can take these jokers.' Who *says* that?"

"Punch line."

"'Let's do the damn thing.'" Greatness reads.

In unison, they say, "slang."

"Who the hell is Jeremy?"

"These are just random."

"That's a narrative line."

"That's a descriptive line, ass! He just described how his ass looked."

"Whatever. Descriptive, narrative, it's the same thing."

"No it's not."

"You gotta describe stuff in order to put it in a story. 'Sometimes a woman got to kill herself to survive.' Now that sounds like some suicidal shit."

"Punch line."

"'My mother hated me, my father disowned me.' That's a line all its own. That's a class of it's own."

"Just put a question mark and we'll come back to it."

"'God, you gave me a brain.'"

"Religious."

"'Hopefully my day will come very soon.' That's a narrative line. 'Everything is both debatable and negotiable.'" Silence. "Put a question mark. Okay, we got all the pages labeled. Now we can do a little bit of brainstorming as to how we can use the lines or where we can use the lines and in what context. And play..." Greatness fiddles with his computer.

When I was little,

"That's the shit!" Truth smiles.

my father was famous.

"Gotta stay awake," Greatness says.

He was the greatest Samurai in the empire,
and he was the Shogun's decapitator.

He cut off the heads of 131 lords.
It was a bad time for the Empire.

"You got something to eat?" Truth asks. "I gotta go to the bathroom."

"What?"

"I'm hungry."

"What? Now."

"Ah, I left my food at home."

"It's in the fridge."

"Oh, you put it in the fridge?"

"I'm not basic." Truth yells something about an ass. "Shut *up*." Greatness lies on his in front of the computer and rests some paper over his face to shield his eyes from the light. After a moment, it slides off.

"Turn it up."

"What?"

"I said, you should turn it back up."

They were supposed to kill my father, but they didn't.
That was the night everything changed.

See, sometimes, you gotta flash 'em back.
See, niggas don't know where this shit started.
Y'all know where it came from,
sayin' we gonna take y'all back to the swords, we bounce, yo.

When the MC's came
to live out their name and to perform,
some had to snort cocaine to act insane
with before Pete Rock-ed it on, now gone,
that the mental plane to spark the brain
with the building to be born,
Yo RZA flip the track with the 'what to' guy
Check em check chicka icka etta UHH
Fake niggas get blitzed and mic bites
I swing swords and cut clowns
Shit is too swift to bite you record and write it down
I flow like the blood on a murder scene, like a syringe

Greatness opens one eye, then both. "Hey, there better not be none of that strippin' up in here, man." He sounds unreasonably paranoid.

"No dude."

But it was yo cock, the shop stolen heart
Catch a swollen heart from not rollin' smart
I put mad pressure, on phony wack rhymes that get hurt
Shit's played, like zodiac signs on sweatshirt
That's minimum, and feminine like sandals
My minimum table stacks a verse on a gamble
Energy is felt once the cards are dealt
With the impact of roundhouse kicks from black belts
that attack, the mic-fones like cyclones or typhoon
I represent from midnight to high noon
I don't waste ink, nigga I think
I drop megaton BOMBS more faster than you blink
Cause rhyme thoughts travel at a tremendous speed
Clouds of smoke, of natural blends of weed
Only under one circumstance is if I'm blunted
Turn that shit up, my clan in da front want it
When the MC's came
to live out their name and to perform
Some had, to snort cocaine to act insane
with before Pete Rock-ed it on, now gone
that the mental plane to spark the brain
with the building to be born
Yo RZA flip the track with the what to guy
Check 'em check chicka icka etta UHH

Truth asks Greatness if he wants any food as he sits down with a Styrofoam take-out container. "No," Greatness says, as Truth jumps up to grab something he left in the kitchen. The moment he's gone, Greatness swipes a bite of something. Truth doesn't seem to notice.

"Okay. In order to write this poem we're going to have to find some similarities between the lines so it flows."

"Like, duh," Truth says between bites.

"You know. Just stating the obvious."

"Alright," Truth begins.

"Similarities. So. Let's start with this page first and try to identify the similarities." He looks at Truth and crinkles his face. "Would you get the fork out your mouth? You look retarded." Truth keeps the fork in his mouth as he rearranges his position, putting his feet near the fire. "All up in my fireplace. Motherfucker wish he had one."

"What page are you on?"

"'Three years ago.'" Truth takes a bite, and Greatness watches as something oozes from his mouth back into the Styrofoam.

"You're such a slop," Greatness says, with disgust.

"What the hell?"

"Slop. Sloppy."

"Three years ago and before the twins were born. Introductory. You know what? The narrative, description, and introductory lines kind of go hand in hand. They can help us develop some kind of way to pull everything together. Like, okay, say for instance you introduce something, and then you describe something. You can describe what you're introducing in order to make it flow."

"That's simple."

"Okay. Let me see. 'Three years ago and before the twins were born.' 'Life in Houston was a bit different.' Because that was before the twins were born."

"Three years ago and before the twins were born, life in Houston was a bit different. Afterward, I began straightening things up around my two-bedroom, two-bathroom condo until my telephone started ringing."

"Telephone started ringing. 'And now the moment you've been waiting for.' To introduce something else."

"Okay. What..."

"Don't get no sauce on my floor."

"Shut up! Alright, what we don't want ... you know what I did notice. What all these lines have in common, or most of them anyway..."

"What's that?"

"They start with 'girl.' So maybe we can talk about girls."

"We should talk to more than just a girl. We should talk to their counterpart too."

"I'm just saying. It seems like the girl's the main character."

Ladies and gentlemen, we'd like to welcome to you
all the way from the slums of Shaolin

Truth belches.

special uninvited guests
came in through the back door
ladies and gentlemen, it's them!

Dance with the mantis, note the slim chances
Chant this, anthem swing like Pete Sampras
Taking it straight to Big Man on Campus
Brandish your weapon or get dropped to the canvas
Scandalous, made the metro panic
Cause static, with or without the automatic
And while I'm at it, yo, you got cash, pass it
It's drastic, gotta send half to Dirty Bastard

Hey yo, hey yo

Waves is spinning, blades is spinning

After a long pause, Greatness speaks up. "Okay so, I mean in order for a woman to have a baby, a man needs to be in the picture, too."

"But I am not going to sit here and do one of those pieces."

"I know, I'm just saying. I'm just stating the obvious. I agree with you." Greatness lies down again.

"Yeah right, fool."

"So who do we want this piece to reach out to?"

"It's got to be universal. I know there's a lot of black themes in here and we could probably take the easy route and do the whole black thing and go somewhere easy with it."

"Maybe we can touch on something that people don't appreciate. Something like a consciousness thing. A wake up."

"I don't want to do that either."

"Not necessarily wake up. Something that help people be more observant." Truth grunts his disapproval. "If we don't do that then we're just being degenerates," Greatness says.

Your socks hangin' out, yours is talkin'
Rock so steadily, son, I'm still crazy
Sport my old Force MD furs in the 80's
Nat Turners wit' burners, Jackie Joyner-Kersee
Taught y'all niggas how to rap, reimburse me
Rothsdale's, ruby red sales, Bloomingdale's, blocks

Ox tails chopped up in Caribbean spots
under these bikini bitches, switchin' with they backs out
Niggas wanna pop shit, I pop clips

In unison, they recite along with the lyrics, "*Bitch,* I'll put my dick on ya lips."

Alabama split, hammer slay quick
That David Banner gamma ray shit
Shells in the mouth, jailhouse snitch
My powder voice, Snow White stiff

"Alright, alright, this is what's up. I want to be able to talk to like, not like, everybody. Even thought you have "she" and all that stuff in here I don't want to take it the whole that route. I don't want it to be a specific character, is what I'm trying to say. I just want it to be, not in general, but ... I don't want it to be a specific character. Like we don't need to be talking specifically *about* someone." He starts humming along with the beat.

"I said that awhile ago," Greatness claims. "Okay, so how are we going to do that."

"It has to be able to speak to all audiences. And you already know how we do, so..." Greatness's eyes are closed. Truth lies down and covers his face with his hat.

Broads on the floor, wall to wall
There's more at the door, players ball to score
'Cause this right here is for all of y'all
Rakim and Primo, yo I got what you need bro
You go see a show, smoke an L, mean yo
And deejays play hits with hard bass kicks
And then they display tricks like The Matrix
Make the record fly undetected by the naked eye
So just feel the vibe 'cause your ears never lie
Nowadays deejays bags of tricks, graphic
On some behind the back shit, catch it and scratch it
Classic, this kid got his craft mastered
Hands is mad quick like he mix with magic
Spin it back and forth and grab it,

and know just where it is ...
There it is.

Hardcore ... real ill niggas
I'm internationally known
When I be on the mic

Hardcore ... real ill niggas
So all hail the honorable

To my elite peeps with the murderous mystiques
I hit the streets with beats and they critique for weeks
They be like "How that kid Ra reach the peak?"
Pull out the heat and use my technique to speak
It's dangerous, sit calm and explain to kids
What part of the game this is in foreign languages
They hold Ra's events in different continents
Put my lyrical contents in monuments
In ghetto garments, I rock a towel like a pharaoh
Mind travel, design style like apparel

"Alright, so, we know it's going to be..." Truth begins, twirling a pen.

Greatness finishes the sentence. "Something for everybody."

"There's got to be something for everybody," Truth agrees.

"Something everybody can see," Greatness says.

"Okay, what about like, philosophy?"

"Something everybody can see," Greatness repeats. "Okay, so let's go with it."

"Okay if it's a philosophy of speaking to everybody, who's the audience? The audience is going to be art critics. People who are very judgmental and shit."

"Coming from us?"

"Like, I don't know ... everybody has their own specific perception of like, this is hard or whatever. So, that being said. So, we know the audience we're trying to get to is like, an art audience and art critics and whatever. But then, we don't want to make it black to the point where they're just like, there goes another nigger poem, and they just going to talk about the struggle and all that bullshit. And then we don't want to sit here and give like, somebody a 'You know better than this' type of speech, or 'You know better than that.' And we don't want to..." He trails off.

> *They break his mom's furniture, watchin'* Comicview
> *Got babies by different ladies high smokin' L's*
> *in the same spot he stood since, eighty-five well*
> *When his stash low, he be crazy*
> *Say he by his moms, hit her on her payday*
> *Junior high school dropout, teachers never cared*
> *They was paid just to show up and leave, no one succeeds*
> *So he moves with his peers, different blocks, different years*
> *Sittin' on, different benches like it's musical chairs*
> *All his peoples moved on in life, he's on the corners at night*
> *with young dudes it's them he wanna be like*
> *It's sad but it's fun to him right? He never grew up*
> *31 and can't give his youth, he's in his second childhood*
> *Cause when I flow the for the street ... who else could it be?*
> *N-A-S*
> *Nas*
> *Resurrect, through the birth of my seed ... Queensbridge*
> *Make everything right ... Get yours, nigga.*

"Okay, okay. What is art?" Truth asks.

"What is art? It's an expression through pictures. But poetry is art that can be interpreted that can't be seen but can be digested and interpreted by the mind."

"You can't feel it physically. So no. So art is something that can be felt mentally, emotionally."

"Yeah.

"So if we did this, if we use all these lines and we're like, 'What is art? Art is so and so and so and so. Blah blah blah. And just come out with the lines.'

"Think about it like this. In this context. You can plan everything like, in terms of life. Life relates to every human being on this planet. Art is life. You can paint a picture of somebody's life. Simple. Well not necessarily simple. But you know. You can't plan everything. I mean you can plan everything but it doesn't necessarily mean that just because you plan it it's going to turn out the way you wanted it to. That's on so many different levels. Like that phrase, 'there's more than one way to skin a cat.' There's no correct format for everything in this world."

"We're coming from left field with this thing."

"Okay, think about this. This phrase I came up with. All my life I've been searching for the perfect stencils to guide my pencils so the images of my existence will be illustrated correctly. Now—"

Truth cuts him off. "Wait, say it again."

"All my life I've been searching for the perfect stencils to guide my pencils so the images of my existence could be illustrated correctly," Greatness reads from his notebook.

"You wrote that for this, or you just had that?"

"I wrote this for this. Cause I mean, think about it. If you want to talk about life, basically life is all about doing the right thing when you're supposed to. Do the right thing when you're supposed to. But sometimes doing the right thing isn't doing the right thing. You have to improvise. And basically the facts of this world—the facts, the stuff that's a constant, that's nothing more than a suggestion of life. And the opinions are basically the choices that us humans make."

"Okay, whoa. Say that again, that line that you just said."

"What, facts are nothing more than...?"

"Yeah."

"Facts are nothing more than life's suggestions, and opinions are the choices that us humans make," Greatness repeats.

"Facts are nothing but life's suggestions, opinions are the choices that we make. Okay, I can rock that. That'd probably be a good philosophy."

"Yeah, we can go philosophical with this thing."

"Okay, so spit the line."

"Which one?"

"The first one. The one that you just wrote."

"All my life I've been searching for the perfect stencils to guide my pencils so the images of my existence could be illustrated correctly."

"Alright. Let's find out what lines we can use to start off with." They flip through their papers for a few seconds. "Got it." Truth crows.

"Already? You'd think you'd do a little brainstorming before you jump into it, but okay. Let me see what you got."

"I got it. Check it out. Follow this line with your first line, alright? Check this out." He clears his throat, then continues, "Many say a dream is a premonition of what the future holds. But as I fought the demons in my nightmare, I prayed not to be the truth."

"All my life I've been searching for the perfect pencils to guide my pencils so that the images of my existence can be illustrated correctly."

"And then we can use the hook."

"What"

"Facts are life's suggestions, the opinions and choices that we make." Truth says.

"TAH," they yell in unison, and slap hands.

"That's what I'm talking about," says Greatness. "So let's write this thing."

"This is going to take forever, isn't it," Truth mutters, as if realizing it for the first time.

"Yeah, basically. The hook we can say together. And that's every time. We hit 'em with a line from this, we hit 'em with something."

"Any line that we use that's going to be basically significant to something. That way we don't run it over."

"There was another line I came across..."

"Let's get this one," Truth interrupts.

"What part?"

"The many saw the dream."

"So you're going to be going first? You're going to start off?"

"What's the first line we're going to be using?"

"Many say the dream is what the future..."

"Okay, so that's your line. I'll come up behind you with my line."

They write in their notebooks.

"The next line that we say together is 'facts are life's suggestions.' What is it?"

"Facts are nothing more than life's suggestions."

"Okay, and opinions are what?"

"Opinions are nothing more than the choices we make."

"Choices we make."

"Going to do something I rarely do: I'm writing on a tablet. I haven't spoken analog in a long, long time. SO now we gotta find our next step, which is—" he picks up his pages "—somewhere in here."

Truth stops him. "Hit it one time so we can see how it sounds."

"Okay."

"Many say a dream is a premonition of what the future holds. But as I fought the demons in my nightmares, I prayed that not to be the truth."

"All my life I've been searching for the perfect stencils to guide my pencils so that the images of my life could be illustrated correctly."

Together: "Facts are nothing more than life's suggestions. Opinions are nothing more than the choices we make."

"Sounds good. Sounds good. Sounds dope."

"That's a good hook line. So we know we going to be using it."

"Yeah I know, we just do that for both." Greatness walks away.

"I'm going to go get something to drink."

"Yep."

* * *

Truth sits motionless, cross-legged, staring silently at his notebook, when Greatness walks in.

"We got the first three lines down," Greatness says as he sits.

"Wait a minute," Truth says, moving. He messes around with the computer.

They say
people come from far, far, far away to find their dreams.

Satisfied, he sits down.

"Okay, we got the first lines down," Greatness repeats. "We just got to pick some lines from here so we can put them in a sequence."

"Of course, but got to write a story in between. We're not just going to take line after line after line," Truth mumbles, a pen in his mouth.

"No stuff."

"Aight," Truth says. "Whose turn, my turn?"

"Uh, yeah."

"Or are you going first?"

"You can go."

Truth mumbles. "They said dreams ... okay wait, read it again so I can catch it. We'll read it from the top again."

"Okay."

Truth begins, a bit stiffly. "Many said a dream is a premonition of what the future holds. But as I fought the demons in my nightmares, I prayed for this not to be true."

"All my life I been searching for the perfect stencils to guide my pencils so that the images of my life can be guided correctly."

Together, "Facts are nothing more than life's suggestions. Opinions are nothing more than the choices we make."

"Okay. So we touched on facts and opinions."

Truth sifts through pieces of paper. "... choices..."

Greatness has an announcement. "The time has finally come for the verdict. That's our narrative line that's going to carry us."

"Something's got to lead up to that."

"That's what I'm *saying*. We got to have a narrative line. I mean, as a matter of fact, let's have a look at all the narrative lines. See which ones we can use toward the beginning, toward the middle, toward the end. Cause we got to narrate throughout."

"That's what I'm saying, man. We'll figure it out as we go through."

"Yeah, that's what I'm saying. We got to look at it now so it will come out correctly." Truth seems to agree; they read separately, silently. "Matter of fact..." Greatness says, "Scratch that." He yawns, and lies down. "Life in Houston was a bit different." It's almost a query.

"I'm going to say some stuff before I say that."

"Okay. Whatever you're going to say, let me know. So I know what line to choose."

"I'm choosing the line."

"You chose the first one." He opens his eyes, looks directly at Truth.

"No I'm saying, if I choose the next line, to lead you to the next line. Like if said, something something something something something, 'Let's do the damn thing.' Then you can do, blah blah blah blah blah blah, 'Hard hit 'em with the strike' or whatever. You know what I'm saying?" Greatness's eyes are closed, and he nods.

California

Greatness sighs. "Okay." He mumbles something. "So we gotta write these, so we can make sure we know what lines we've already used." He pauses. "We haven't used but one line." He looks up at Truth. "Shut up." And then, "Okay, so what are you going to say?"

"I don't know! Shut up," Truth says, without looking up.

"Hurry *up*."

Truth mumbles something about a hook, and Greatness assents. "The hook is in the lines we have," Greatness affirms.

Let's trace the hints and check the file
Let see who bit to detect the style
I flip the script so they can't get foul
At least not now, it'll take a while
I change the pace to complete the beat
I drop the bass 'til MC's get weak
For every word they trace, it's a scar they keep
'Cause when I speak, they freak to sweat the technique

I made my debut in '86
Wit' a melody and a president's mix
And now I stay on target and refuse to miss
And I still make hits
With beats, parties, clubs in the cars and jeeps
My underground sound vibrates the streets
MC's wanna beef then I play for keeps
When they sweat the technique

Don't sweat the technique

"Dealing with cars too much," Greatness says. Truth laughs. "Death is just collecting dust."

Pencils and pens are swords
Letters put together form a key to chords
I'm also a sculpture born with structure
Because of my culture I'm a rip and destruct the
Difficult styles that'll be for the technology
Complete sights and new heights after I get deep
You don't have to speak just seek
And peep the technique

But don't sweat the technique

I speak indiscreet 'cause talk is cheap
Then I get deep and the weak then complete their
Pull with a seat, never weak or obsolete
They never grow old techniques become antiques
Better then something brand new 'cause it's radiant
And the wild style'll have much more volume

Classical too intelligent to be radical
Masterful, never irrelevant mathematical
Here's some soothing souvenirs for all the years
They fought and sought, the thoughts and ideas
It's cool when you freak to the beat
But don't sweat the technique

Don't sweat the technique

"I think there might be a link," Greatness says, "between this line and this line. I might be able to use those in conjunction if whatever you say, like, it totally depends on what you say whether I can use those lines together. Cause what I'm thinking, it might be able to work.

"Cause right now like, just this one thing alone, we touch on the past and the present, premonitions of the future, the difference between good and evil, presets and improv, facts and opinions, suggestions and choices. So far we've touched on that. We haven't written but like three lines." Greatness waits. "Do you have any idea?"

"Yeah—um," Truth says immediately.

you was trouble right from the start
taught me so many lessons
How not to mess with broken hearts, so many questions
When this began we was the

Greatness joins in: "perfect match."

perhaps
we had some problems but we workin' at it, and now
the arguments are gettin' loud, I wanna stay
But I can't help from walkin' out just throw it away
Just take my hand and understand, if you could see
I never planned to be a man it just wasn't me
But now I'm searchin' for commitment, in other arms
I wanna shelter you from harm, don't be alarmed
Your attitude was the cause, you got me stressin'
Soon as I open up the door with your jealous questions
Like where can I be you're killin' me with your jealousy
Now my ambition's to be free
I can't breathe, cause soon as I leave, it's like a trap
I hear you callin' me to come back,

"What we won't do," Greatness sings along, as Truth lies down, concentrating.

Do for love.
You tried everything,
but you don't give up.

Truth sits back up, mumbling.

Just when I thought I broke away and I'm feelin' happy
You try to trap me say you pregnant and guess who the daddy
Don't wanna fall for it, but in this case what could I do? So now I'm back
to makin' promises to you, tryin' to keep it true
What if I'm wrong, a trick to keep me holding on
Tryin' to be strong and in the process, keep you goin'
I'm bout to lose my composure, I'm gettin' close
To packin' up and leavin' notes, and gettin' ghost
Tell me who knows, a peaceful place where I can go
To clear my head I'm feelin' low, losin' control
My heart is sayin' leave, oh what a tangled web we weave
when we conspire to conceive, and now
You gettin' calls at the house, guess you cheatin'
That's all I need to hear cause I'm leavin', I'm out the do'
Never no more will you see me, this is the end
Cause now I know you've been cheatin', I'm a sucka...

What you won't do
Do for love

Greatness is tired of waiting. "Okay?" he says, expectantly.

"Okay," Truth responds, and begins writing in his notebook. Greatness's hands follow his fingers for a minute.

Now he left you with scars, tears on your pillow and you still stay
As you sit and pray, hoping the beatings'll go away
It wasn't always a hit and run relationship
It use to be love, happiness and companionship
Remember when I treated you good
I moved you up to hills, out the ills of the ghetto hood
Me and you a happy home, when it was on
I had a love to call my own
I shoulda seen you was trouble but I was lost, trapped in your eyes
Preoccupied with gettin' tossed, no need to lie
You had a man and I knew it, you told me
Don't worry bout it we can do it now I'm under pressure
Make a decision cause I'm waitin', when I'm alone

I'm on the phone havin' secret conversations, huh
I wanna take your misery, replace it with happiness
but I need your faith in me, I'm a sucka for love
sucka for love, know you ain't right G but yet I'm a sucka for love

Greatness lies on his elbow, head facing the computer. It is impossible to tell if he is sleeping.

Truth steps up. "Oh shit," he says, excited.

"What?"

Truth looks from his notebook to the printed pages, then back to his notebook. He writes quickly and deliberately.

I sip the Dom P, watchin' Gandhi til' I'm charged
Then writin' in my book of rhymes, all the words pass the margin
To hold the mic I'm throbbin', mechanical movement
Understandable smooth shit that murderers move wit'
The thief's theme, play me at night, they won't act right
The fiend of hip-hop has got me stuck like a crack pipe
The mind activation, react like I'm facin' time like
'Pappy' Mason with pens I'm embracin'
Wipe the sweat off my dome, spit the phlegm on the streets
Suede Timbs on my feets, makes my cypher complete
Whether cruisin' in a six-cab, or Montero Jeep
I can't call it, the beats make me fallin' asleep
I keep fallin', but never fallin' six feet deep
I'm out for presidents to represent me (Say what?)
I'm out for presidents to represent me (Say what?)
I'm out for dead presidents to represent me
"It's yours!"
Whose world is this?
The world is yours, the world is yours.
It's mine, it's mine, it's mine.
Whose world is this?
"It's yours!"
It's mine, it's mine, it's mine.
Whose world is this?
The world is yours, the world is yours
It's mine, it's mine, it's mine.
Whose world is this?
To my man Ill Will, God bless your life

"It's yours!"
To my peoples throughout Queens, God bless your life
I trip we box up crazy bitches aimin' guns in all my baby pictures
Beef with housin' police, release scriptures that's maybe Hitler's
Yet I'm the mild, money gettin' style, rollin' foul
The versatile, honey stickin' wild, golden child
Dwellin' in the Rotten Apple, you get tackled
Or caught by the devil's lasso, shit is a hassle
There's no days, for broke days, we sell it, smoke pays
While all the old folks pray, to Jesus' soakin' they sins in trays
of holy water, odds against Nas are slaughter
Thinkin' a word best describin' my life, to name my daughter

Truth sits up. "Tag, bitch!"

My strength, my son, the star, will be my resurrection

Greatness is snarling. "Don't touch me."

Born in correction all the wrong shit I did, he'll lead a right direction

Truth, louder. "Tag, bitch!"

"Read it," Greatness says.

"Alright, check it out."

Greatness mutters, "Idiot."

Truth flips through sheets of paper, "Here we go, here we go." Then he pauses. "So, okay. Start from your line. Read it."

Greatness is grumpy. "I don't want to read it."

Truth isn't having it. "Yeah, yeah. Read it. Your line."

"All my life I've been searching for the perfect stencils to guide my pencil so that the images of my life could be illustrated correctly," Greatness begins.

Together, they say, "Facts are nothing more than life's suggestions. Opinions are nothing more than the choices we make."

"But the world runs on paparazzi perceptions and get rich quick schemes. Kids wanna grow up. Adults wanna get money. And that's before the eyes are allowed to gasp air and catch its breath. There's absolutely nothing slow about me but the way I walk.

"Tag, bitch. Tag. Tag."

"Shut up."

"Tag."

"Shut up." As Greatness looks at his notebook, Truth gets up and walks toward the kitchen.

Born alone, die alone, no crew to keep my crown or throne
I'm deep by sound alone

"Whose Sprite is this?" Truth asks.

I need a new nigga, for this black cloud to follow
Cause while it's over me it's too dark to see tomorrow

After a moment, Greatness responds. "That's mine." Then he adds, generously. "But you can have some."

"There you go."

... I flip, fill the clip to the tip
Picturin my peeps, now the income make my heartbeat skip
And I'm amped up, they locked the champ up, even my brain's in handcuffs
Headed for Indiana stabbin' women like the Phantom
The crew is lampin' big Willie style
Check the chip toothed smile, plus I profile wild
Stash through the flock wools, burnin' dollars to light my stove
Walk the blocks wit' a bop, checkin' Danes plus the games people play, bust the problems of the world today
"It's yours!"
"It's mine, it's mine, it's mine.
Whose world is this?
The world is yours, the world is yours.
It's mine, it's mine, it's mine.
Break it down.
To everybody in Queens, the foundation
The world is yours
To everybody uptown, yo, the world is yours
The world is yours
To everybody in Brooklyn
Y'all know the world is yours
Everybody in Mount Vernon, the world is yours

Long Island, the world is yours
Staten Island, yeah the world is yours
South Bronx, the world is yours

Greatness hasn't stopped writing. He writes slowly, steadily, deliberately, brows furrowed. The computer screen fades to black, even as the music continues. In the other room, the water is running.

He walks outside for a cigarette break,
and thinks how many cigarettes does it take
he takes a long drag with the sun in his eye
he squints, he thinks, he starts to sigh
sometimes he cry
when he thinks about his girlfriend on his side
she held him down
she made him better
For the love fucked up weather
and she thinkin' about the life
with no more work just being the wife
but instead, her love she gave it to a man
who fought against her lovely plans
so when she goes to work
plus go to school
plus fight for love she must feel like a fool
she want the ease to come after pain
she fights for love that's her campaign

We fight. We love.

"Tag!" Greatness says. He looks for Truth. "Get your ass over here. Quit drinking out of my wine glass."

"Shut up."

"I don't come over your house and fuck up your shit."

"Yeah right!" Truth laughs.

"And then you're just going to bring it over here? Disrespecting me motherfucker." Truth sits down, wine glass in hand. "Alright, read off your line."

"The world runs on paparazzi perceptions and get rich quick schemes. Kids wanna grow up, Adults wanna get money. And that's before their eyes are allowed to gasp air and catch its breath. There's absolutely nothing slow about me but the way I walk."

Greatness: "In the opposite direction facing forward, like everyone else who thinks they can step into yesterday and re-live today and tomorrow differently. But today is already happening—maybe in a different universe, but life in Houston was a bit different, so there was no use dwelling on shit I can't change."

"You used two lines," Truth says, scratching his head.

"Yeah. Fucked with it," Greatness says.

It's Truth's turn. He kicks something loud, over and over again, taps his pen against the carpet, rhythmically pulls his t-shirt away from his arm.

You make me step my game up.

"Mark off the lines that we've used," Greatness says, handing Truth several pieces of paper. Truth has a green highlighter and black pen in one hand and a blue pen in the other.

"Read your line again," Truth asks.

Greatness articulates. "In the opposite direction..." He pauses. "Oh wait, um. You said your last line was the way you walk?"

"The way I walk."

"I meant to say backwards." He jots something down. "Backwards in the opposite direction, facing forward like everyone, else who thinks, they can step into yesterday and re-live today and tomorrow differently, but today is already happening, maybe in a different universe, but life in Houston was a bit different, so there was no use dwelling on shit I can't change."

You make me step my game up.

"Your last line?" Truth asks.

"There was no use in me dwelling on shit I can't change."

"That's what we put in the hook," he says.

"Huh?"

"That's what we put in the hook. Facts are nothing more than life's suggestions. Opinions are nothing more than the choices we make."

"Okay," Greatness gets it.

They write.

Even the sun goes down.
Heroes eventually die.

Greatness has to remind Truth that it's his turn. Greatness sits up, sneezes, recites, "go get your work and keep your beeper chirpin' is a must ... sack man ... that man ... I'm strapped man & ready to bust on any nigga like that man ... like Batman, and Robin..." He doodles in the corner of his page and yawns for a full four seconds. Truth concentrates.

Twice upon a time there was a boy who died twice
and lived happily ever after but that's another chapter
live from home of the brave with dirty dollars
and beauty parlors and baby ballers and bowling ball Impalas
and street scholars that's majoring in culinary arts
You know how to work bread cheese and dough
from scratch but see the catch is you can get caught
Know what ya sellin' what ya bought so cut that big talk
Let's walk to the bridge now meet me halfway
now you may see some children dead off in the pathway
it's them poor babies walkin' slowly to the candy lady
It's lookin' bad need some hope
like the words maybe, if, or probably more than a hobby
when my turntables get wobbly they don't fall
I'm sorry y'all I often drift I'm talkin' gift
so when it comes you never look the horse inside it's grill
of course you know I feel like the bearer of bad news
Don't want to be it but it's needed so what have you
Now question is every nigga with dreads for the cause?
Is every nigga with golds for the fall? Naw.

Truth and Greatness keeping writing.

Alien can blend right on in wit' yo' kin
look again 'cause I swear I spot one every now & then

Bored, Greatness walks away to grab a magazine and Truth tries his line quietly, moving his hand in rhythm with the lines. Greatness flips through the pages and pauses on a spread: a white car is surrounded by gold text, staring intently. He occasionally glances up at

Truth, and finally says. "A watch that costs sixteen thousand dollars. Are you serious?" It's a rhetorical question, and Truth doesn't look up.

Let's go to sleep in Paris,
and wake up in Tokyo.
Have a dream in New Orleans,
fall in love in Chicago.
Wherever I go she goes.

"Tag, bitch," Truth says, a bit more gently than the last time.

"Read it." Greatness is withholding judgment.

"Tag."

"Read it."

"Alright, read the hook real quick." Truth counts off: "1 ... 2 ... 3..." and then recites "Cause facts are nothing more than life's suggestions" while Greatness says "Cause facts are nothing more than life's situations." They hear they clash. "Suggestions," Truth corrects him. "Where did you get situations from?" Greatness shrugs.

They recite in unison this time: "Cause facts are nothing more than life's suggestions. Cause opinions are nothing more than the choices we make," then Truth continues, "Ask a family with a male child how they feel about their future, and they'll say, 'We used to be so happy, when our country believed in Isolationism, but ever since reasons can be satisfied using zero tolerance by any means necessary distortions, the separation between government ideology and the American dream has boiled down to one question to achieve success, 'Can you be a good soldier and help out a general?'" He throws down his pen. "*Tag.*"

"Shut up," Greatness says quietly, as Truth stands up and dances a little jig.

"Tag, man. Tag!"

"Shut up." Greatness begins to write.

Truth helps himself to more Sprite, then comes back to his spot. Using his notebook as a pillow, he covers his face with his hat and attempts to go to sleep. He hasn't lay for more than two minutes before Greatness throws his pen to his paper. "Tag." Truth doesn't move. Greatness swats the hat off Truth's face. "Tag."

"Read it," Truth says, picking the hat up and putting it back over his eyes.

"Read your last line," Greatness says.

Truth gets up. "the separation between government ideology and the American dream has boiled down to one question to achieve success, 'Can you be a good soldier and help out a general?"

"The type of general that monologues about his own successful acquisition of the American dream, and just like everyone else, I'm sick and tired of hearing the same ole story without being a part of it,

sick of the same shit different day routine, so I started living each day as if it were my last. This feeling is too familiar: that dream ... it's starting again. That same dream."

"We're supposed to chop that one up, huh."

"Mmm."

"I said, we're supposed to chop that one up, huh?"

"Chop it up," Greatness tells him. "Unless I can just take—"

"—Shut up," Truth cuts him off sharply. He's tired.

"Whatever," Greatness brushes it off, turning the music up.

Ladies and gentlemen,
Wanna welcome y'all back to "The Minstrel Show"
Thank y'all for tuning in; y'all keep watching a lotta the station
But y'all touring us right now
And it feels so beautiful
Performing at black face tonight!
It's my nigga, Joe Scudda
Coming up a little bit later on in the show
I just wanna thank y'all for just tuning in

It's like this yo...
Yo, when 'te pulls his verses out
Promoters pull their purses out.

Truth turns to the previous page in his notebook, silently re-reads the last line, then turns back to a new, blank page. He kneels over his notebook, then lies on his stomach, carefully placing the cap on the green pen while keeping the red one between his teeth. It isn't Greatness's turn, but he continues to write.

Life's a battle.
Mean streets eat you alive.
Blocks'll have you,
tryin' to maintain your course through the potholes and gravel.

Greatness wakes the computer from its sleep and gazes at the playlist.

Gotta get away. Some try but head back.
Street-smart niggas got left back.
Some died; they left stacks.
Me, I be alright, and on top of that I'm dog nice.
Jigga been cold as fuck before ice.
Not before Christ, but a long fuckin' time.
Get your mind right niggas.

Greatness picks up the magazine again. Truth shifts position and writes, then shifts position again, writes some more. He balances on his knees and elbows. He is left-handed. The song changes again.

Watch these rap niggas get all up in your guts
French-vanilla, butter-pecan, chocolate-deluxe
Even caramel sundaes is gettin' touched
And scooped in my ice cream truck, Wu tears it up
(The ice cream man is coming!)
Yo honey-dips, summertime, fine Jheri drippin'
See you on Pickens with a bunch of chickens how you're clickin'
I catch shootin' strong notes as we got close
She rocked rope, honey throat smellin' like Impulse
Your whole shell baby's wicked like Nimrod
Caught me like a fresh-water scrod, or may I not be God
Attitude is very rude Boo, crabby like seafood
It turns me on like Vassey and Lahrule
They call me Starky Love-hun, check the strategy
By any means, Shirley Temple cross was done by Billie Jean's
Black Mrs. America, your name is Erica, right true
Lazy eyeball, small piece, six shoe
Caramel complexion, breath smellin' like cinnamon

For minutes, Truth's hand is the only thing in the room that moves. Then, Greatness turns the pages of his magazine, faster and faster until he throws the whole thing toward the fireplace and leaves the room. Truth continues to write.

* * *

By the time Greatness enters the room, Truth is doodling. He looks up when Greatness sits down. "Tag, bitch," he says. "Tag. Tag."

"What you got?"

"Alright. Read your last line."

"This feeling is too familiar. That dream. It's starting again. That dream."

"It's starting again. But before I go any further, allow me to introduce myself as 'that dream,' or at least that's what we've been told to become. That same dream. Where the only reason no one blames you for failing is because no one else has completely succeeded. And now, the moment you've been waiting for: Yes, we're black males spitting poetry, trying to educate those of worldly struggles and not of what's going on in 'the hood.' Cause in your mind right now, your soul is telling you: 'we don't need another nigga eatin' off our plate.'" His tone turns sing-song—"Wait for it..." and then reverts—"Greatness, and you say 'what?' 'I didn't get an answer.'

"Oh, and when I say, 'and now, the moment you've been waiting for,' we both say 'Yes, we're black males spitting poetry, trying to educate those of worldly struggles and not of what's going on in 'the hood.' Cause in your mind right now, your soul is telling you: we don't need another nigga eatin' off our plate. Wait for it...' And then I'll be like, 'Greatness!' And you're like, 'what?' And I'll say, 'I didn't get an answer.'"

Greatness mumbles his assent as he begins to write his part. He looks too tired to argue. Truth highlights something on another piece of paper.

"And you can come in with a good line right here," Truth tells him. "Why you so worried about it? I got this. Pow. Yeah?"

"Yeah," Greatness almost manages a smile.

Down south where we buy them hammers
Down south where we sell them drugs
Down south where life is cheap
where they quick to fill you up with slugs

"You like how I chopped and screwed that line? I chopped that line up." Truth smiles as Greatness rubs his eyes.

"What lines did you use?"

" 'Didn't get an answer.' 'And now the moment you've been waiting for.' " He keeps flipping through. "Oh yeah, cause I chopped and screwed the other line. So I just used two."

"And now the moment we've been looking for. We don't need another nigga eating off our plate. I didn't get a answer." He sings along with Talib Kweli: "Shit, the rest is history."

"Oh yeah," Truth says. "When you come in with 'why you so worried about it, I got this,' you can be like, 'we can take these jokers.' We can both be like, 'we can take these jokers.' Like, write something in there so we can be like, 'we can take these jokers.'"

Greatness nods, still singing along with the song. "Short Dog is my O.G., we been down forever. Taught me the game, lane to lane, and keep my pimpin' together."

Truth lays down, head on notebook, and covers his face with his hat. After a moment, he joins the song too. "Starving blacks on the news, I weighed. Cause we isolate ourselves and give our ghetto pass away. My niggas passed away at an unreal rate."

Greatness continues "with my mic in my hand ... new world clan ... man would ... my hood..." He trails off, deep in thought. "He was just alive. Two years ago."

"He's been dead two years now?" They're discussing the rapper, Pimp C.

"Might have been a little bit more."

"Little bit less, don't you think?"

"Give or take a month or so." He paused. "He died in January 2000 ... naw."

"He died in '08."

"Oh, he died in '08?"

"Yeah."

A nigga that's from the A-Town see
The home of the Bankhead Bounce, Campbellton Road and other city streets
Enough of the verality, fallacy, butter we speak not fiction
Speakin' of pullin' yo' girl lookin' at Jheri curls you bitches
Everytime I rhyme for y'all, I'm lookin' to prove a point
kickin' a freestyle every now and then
but mostly off the joint
See I smoke good cause see it go good wit' them flows, why
the nigga the B-I-G like Tony Rich nobody knows why
but me and my folks, cause y'all niggas jokes just like the joker
I'm sick of these wack ass rappers like I'm tired of hoes in chokers

Truth is motionless as Greatness begins to write.

This ol' sucka MC stepped up to me
Challenged Andre to a battle and I stood there patiently
As he spit and stumbled over clichés, so called freestylin'
On purpose just to make me feel low, I guess you wilin'
I say look Boi, I ain't for that fuck shit; so fuck this
Let me explain on this child style so you don't miss
I grew up to myself not round no park bench
just a nigga bustin' flows off in apartments

Greatness writes in earnest. A phone buzzes. Truth reaches for it without opening his eyes. He slides the hat above his to check the phone, then replaces it.

When I first met my Spottieottiedopaliscious Angel
I can remember that damn thing like yesterday
The way she moved reminded me of a Brown Stallion
horse with skates on smooth like a hot comb
on nappy ass hair
I walked up on her & was almost paralyzed
her neck was smelling sweeter
than a plate of yams with extra syrup
eyes beaming like four karats apiece just blindin' a nigga
felt like I chiefed a whole O of that Presidential
My heart was beating so damn fast
never knowing this moment would bring another
life into this world

Truth is snoring. Greatness consults a piece of paper, then another, then writes, then reviews what he has written and decides that it is acceptable.

"Tag." Greatness looks at Truth. Truth doesn't move. Greatness moves for the hat but Truth, sensing the imminent interruption, stops him mid-movement.

"Read it," Truth says.

"Why you so worried about it? I got this. We can take these jokers. Damn, seems like the shoe is on the other foot now. You made a mistake, so I'm calling your cellular phone, introducing myself as Mr. Consequence with a follow-up text message stating that if you still wanna come, I still wanna see you. Step to my front door because you know I'm getting ready to make a move and when I do, I got you. Like a reaction to an action, back when you were actin' like we had it all. This is Mr. Consequence and I don't want you to come tomorrow. I want you to come now."

"Alright. Which ones did you use?"

"I don't want you to come tomorrow ... used to be so happy ... had it all."

"I already said 'we used to be so happy.'"

"Where?" Greatness asks, as Truth begins to look. "Did you already say 'had it all?' 'We had it all?'"

"How they feel about their future, and they'll say 'we used to be so happy, when our country believed in isolationism.'"

"We used to be so happy? Okay."

"We had it all," Truth is still reading.

"Wait, you used 'we had it all' too?"

"No."

"You used it or I did?"

"You just used it."

"I don't want you to come tomorrow. You know I'm getting ready to make a move, and when I do, I got you."

"Is that it?"

"Uh huh."

"Read it to me again."

"Oh damn, seems like the shoe is on the other foot."

"Word. What else?"

"What are you worried about? I got this."

"Why you so worried? I got this."

"Yeah."

"You got to say it just like it's written."

"Okay."

"Is that it?"

"Yeah."

"Didn't you have something with 'she' in it?"

"No."

"Okay, read it to me then."

"Why you so worried about it? I got this. We can take these jokers. Damn, seems like the shoe is on the other foot now. You made a mistake, so I'm calling your cellular phone, introducing myself as Mr. Consequence with a follow-up text message stating that if you still wanna come, I still wanna see you. Step to my front door because you know I'm getting ready to make a move and when I do, I got you. Like a reaction to a action, back when you were actin' like we had it all. This is Mr. Consequence and I don't want you to come tomorrow. I want you to come now." Finished, he lays down and pulls his t-shirt over his eyes.

Don't everybody like the smell of gasoline?
Well burn motherfucka burn American Dream
Don't everybody like the taste of Apple Pie?
We'll snap for your slice of life I'm tellin' ya why
I hear that mother nature's now on birth control
The coldest pimp be looking for somebody to hold
The highway up to Heaven got a crook on the toll
Youth full of fire ain't got nowhere to go nowhere to go

Truth repeats, maybe to himself, "I don't want you to come tomorrow. I want you to come tonight."

Greatness gets up. Truth writes.

So fuck what you thought
I'm drinkin' Hennessey,
runnin' from my enemies.
Will I live to be 23?
There's so much pain.

Tired of the strain and the pain.
Tired of the strain and the pain.

Truth pauses. He says something to himself. He writes. He scratches his head and writes. He looks at another page, copies something, writes more.

Sky is the limit and you know that you keep on
Just keep on pressin' on
Sky is the limit and you know that you can have what you want, be what you want
Sky is the limit and you know that you keep on
Just keep on pressin' on

Sky is the limit and you know that you can have what you want,
be what you want, have what you want, be what you want

Greatness is gone, who knows where. Truth has been alone, writing, for what seems like a very long time. The music stops for the first time in ages. Truth sighs. "Tag."

"Read it," Greatness says as he sits down. Then he adds, "Don't read it too loud."

"Hmm?"

"Don't read it too loud. My sister's asleep."

"Okay. What's your last line?"

"This is Mr. Consequence and I don't want you to come tomorrow. I want you to come now."

"See, I started living each day as if it were my last—"

Greatness cuts him off. "I used that line already."

"You did? Where?"

"I told you to mark yours. See." He begins to read. "The type of general that monologues about his own successful acquisition of the American dream, and just like everyone else, I'm sick and tired of hearing the same ole story without being a part of it, sick of the same shit different day routine, so I started living each day as if it were my last. This feeling is too familiar: that dream ... it's starting again. That same dream."

"What was your last line again?"

"This is Mr. Consequence and I don't want you to come tomorrow. I want you to come now."

Truth pauses for a moment. "Oh, okay. I got it."

Greatness turns the computer back on.

Sentence begins indented with formality
My duration's infinite, moneywise or physiology
Poetry, that's a part of me, retardedly bop
I drop the ancient manifested hip-hop, straight off the block

Truth says, "Okay, read it again."

"I don't want you to come tomorrow. I want you to come now." Greatness sounds tired.

"Cause tomorrow's not promised. God is good but there has to be a universal understanding that came from nothing and having nothing are two different things. Yeah, I came from nothing, but I was determined to have it all. And how couldn't I? Greatness, it's a trip. Cause everything was both debatable and negotiable. But after the greetings which were transparent from the start, our critics, who watched us closely, yes, they all resumed back to what they were doing before I walked up. So hopefully my day will come very soon. Too much? Greatness. Wait for it. Let's do the damn thing."

Greatness looks confused. "Let's do the damn thing" he murmurs, crossing it out on his page. "Hopefully my day will come very soon. I came from nothing."

"There's no use on dwelling on shit I can't change."

"Everything was both debatable and negotiable."

"God is good."

"What else?"

They are silent. "How many pages have you written?"

"In terms of Greatness I've written one and a quarter. In terms of Truth I've written six."

"That's about right."

"Tree-killing thought process." Greatness shakes his head.

"Let's read it all the way from the top and see how it sounds."

Greatness looks unconvinced. "Not yet." Truth doesn't argue. "Read your last line."

"So hopefully my day will come very soon. Greatness? Wait for it. Let's do the damn thing."

"Okay, read the whole thing."

"Cause tomorrow's not promised. Yes, God is good but there has to be a universal understanding that came from nothing and having nothing are two different things. Yeah, I came from nothing, but I was determined to have it all. And how couldn't I? Greatness, it's a trip, cause everything was both debatable and negotiable. But after the greetings which were transparent from the start, our critics, who watched us closely, yes, they all resumed back to what they were doing *before* I walked up. So hopefully my day will come very soon. Too much? Greatness. Wait for it. Let's do the damn thing."

Dance with the mantis, note the slim chances
Chant this, anthem swing like Pete Sampras
Takin' it straight to Big Man On Campus
Brandish your weapon or get dropped to the canvas
Scandalous, made the metro panic
Cause static, with or without the automatic

And while I'm at it, yo, you got cash, pass it
It's drastic, gotta send half to Dirty Bastard

Truth uses his pen to count something on his paper. "Oh, and everything is both debatable and negotiable."

"Yeah, I got that," Greatness says.

"You could start off with 'God gave me a brain.'"

"You going to have to chop that line up. Cause part of that line isn't ready yet. It's a chop. A religious line. Okay, wait a minute. It *is* ready. It *is* ready." He begins writing.

Yo, you may catch me in a pair of Polo Skipperys, matching cap
Razor blades in my gums (BOBBY!)
You may catch me in yellow Havana Joe's goose jumper
And my phaser off stun (BOBBY!)
Y'all might just catch me in the park playin' chess, studyin' math
Signin' 7 and a sun (BOBBY!)
But you won't catch me without the ratchet, in the joint
Smoked out, dead broke or off point (BOBBY!)
Wallo's comfortable, chocolate frosting
Your socks hangin' out, yours is talkin'
Rock so steadily, son, I'm still crazy
Sport my old Force MD furs in the 80's
Nat Turners wit' burners, Jackie Joyner-Kersee
Taught y'all niggas how to rap, reimburse me
Rothsdale's, ruby red sales, Bloomingdale's, blocks
Ox tails chopped up in Caribbean spots
I'm nice, maxed out, creepin' wit' the ax out
Murder these bikini bitches, switchin' with they backs out

Niggas wanna pop shit, I pop clips
Bitch, I'll put my dick on ya lips
Alabama split, hammer slay quick
That David Banner gamma ray shit
Shells in the mouth, jailhouse snitch
My powder voice, Snow White stiff
Verbal killas, gorilla grip
God body shit, puff Marley spliffs

You might see me in a 6, that's not my style
You might see me wit' a bitch, that's not my child

Truth has an idea. "Oh, I got another thing. Right after you say that line, I can intervene and—"

"God damn." Greatness throws down his pen; he has lost his train of thought.

"Oh." Truth pauses. "My bad."

"No. What is it?"

"I was going to say, you can say, 'God, you gave me a brain, courage, and a heart. Tell me which one to use first before I kill both of these fools.' And after you say that, I jump in and say, 'Nard hit him with the strike of magic and poof, just like that, Jeremy was gone.' Like, you just killed my friend. I'm going to have to chop and screw it though."

"Go ahead and use it. But don't chop it."

"Don't chop it?"

"Don't chop it. It's almost like comic relief. I'm going to act like I have a gun in my hand or whatever, and then like after I finish saying I'm a kill both of these fools, I'm going to go into a freeze frame, and then you jump in and be like, whatever the fuck, Jeremy disappeared or some shit. I'm a be freeze frame, and you just going to step in. Like Afro-Samurai. He was frozen, then Samuel L. Jackson started running his mouth and shit. Like that." Greatness copies, writes, while Truth plays with his phone.

"We still have to do something with all these women lines to use," Truth points out.

To my comrades that keep it flaming hot
On dangerous blocks, claiming spots
Where the goal is to be one of the top-ranked soldiers
Forty-five holders, one of the high rollers
Get respect in the hood, credit is good
Knock it down lumberjack style, baby, extra wood
Rock it all night long, the bang-a-thon baby
Keep hanging on, we like it with the lights on
Don't have to blow twenty thou' to get to know honey's style
Show her the town, steal her heart, no money down

How about some hardcore, yeah we like it raw for sure
Broads on the floor, wall to wall

There's more at the door, players ball to score
'Cause this right here is for all of y'all
Rakim and Primo, yo I got what you need bro
You go see a show, smoke an L, mean yo
And deejays play hits with hard bass kicks
And then they display tricks like The Matrix
Make the record fly undetected by the naked eye
So just feel the vibe 'cause your ears never lie
Nowadays deejays bags of tricks, graphic
On some behind the back shit, catch it and scratch it
Classic, this kid got his craft mastered
Hands is mad quick like he mix with magic
Spin it back and forth and grab it, and know just where it is...

"I know. I figured with the women lines I was just going to refer to poetry." Truth sits up and digs through his backpack.

"You got a Bible?"

"Huh?"

"You got a bible?"

"Yeah.

"Mine's in the car."

"Yeah." Greatness sighs.

To my elite peeps with the murderous mystiques
I hit the streets with beats and they critique for weeks
They be like "How that kid Ra reach the peak?"
Pull out the heat and use my technique to speak
It's dangerous, sit calm and explain to kids
What part of the game this is and foreign languages
They hold Ra's events in different continents
Put my lyrical contents in monuments
In ghetto garments, I rock a towel like a pharaoh
Mind travel, design style like apparel
My fashions last long as a lifetime
Cause I can see the future when the god write rhymes
They're mad cause I managed to reign so long
Like their chance to make money done came and gone
This is strictly for my listeners on the corners at night
And the sisters that be keeping this right, when I be on the mic

Yo
Explode, my thoughts were drunken from quarts of beers
Was years back, before Nasir would explore a career in rap
As a music dude, I mastered this Rubik's Cube
Godzilla, fought Gargantua, eyes glued to the tube
Was a, long time ago, John Boy Ice
Geronimo po-lice jumpin' out Chryslers, easywider paper
Pops puffin' his sess, punchin' his chest like a gorilla
Outside was psychos, killers
Saw Divine, Goon and Chungo, Lil' Turkey
R.I.P. Tyrone, 'member no cursin' front of Ms. Vercey
Big Percy, Crazy Paul, the Sledge Sisters
My building was 40-16, once in the blue, hallways was clean
I knew, all that I'd seen had meant somethin'
Learned early, to fear none little Nas was huntin'
Livin' carefree laughin', got jokes on the daily
Y'all actin' like some old folks y'all don't hear me
Yo I'm in my second childhood
"Cause when I flow for the street..."
"... who else could it be"
"N-A-S"
"Nas..."
"Resurrect, through the birth of my seed..."
"Queensbridge"
"Make everything right..."
"Get yours, nigga"

They both think for a moment. "We should set it up like a run-through," Truth says. "Like, 'I can't stand something-something-something.'"

Greatness looks up.

"Like—" and he started speaking very fast "—'Sometimes a woman had to kill herself to survive.' 'My mother hated me. My father disowned me. Stepfather molested me. Johns used me. Ex-husbands abused me.'"

"Yeah, we can do that," Greatness agreed.

"Okay."

"We gotta do that. That's the only way it's going to work without looking gay."

"Okay."

So he moves with his peers, different blocks, different years
Sittin' on, different benches like it's musical chairs
All his peoples moved on in life, he's on the corners at night
with young dudes it's them he wanna be like
It's sad but it's fun to him right? He never grew up
31 and can't give up his youth, he's in his second childhood.

"I found the final line, too," Truth says. "He whispered as he stretched getting out of bed, 'one more mutherfucking time.'" Greatness raises his eyebrows. He's impressed. "That's deep, right?" They slap hands.

Time flyin' she the same person, never matures
All her friends married doin' well
She's in the streets yakkety yakkin' like she was 12
Honey is twenty-seven, argues fights
Selfish in her own right, for life, guess she's in her second childhood

"The truth is that like, I'm mad I'm not going to be able to make it to that damn party."

"What party?" Truth doesn't sound very interested. Greatness shrugs. "She was like, 'y'all *suck*.'" He pauses. "And I was like, 'I know. You can beat me up for it later.'"

"You used that line 'Same shit, different day,' didn't you?"

"Yeah. I took care of that a long time ago." As Truth highlights his page with the green highlighter, Greatness sounds a bit smug. "See what I mean?"

"Shut the fuck up," Truth mutters calmly.

Against the canvas of the night
Appears a curious celestial phenomena
called Black Star, but what is it?

Black people unite and let's all get down
We got to have what? We got to have that love
What is the Black Star?
Is it the cat with the black shades, the black car?
Is it shinin' from very far, to where you are?
It is commonplace and different

Intimate and distant
Fresher than an infant

Black, my family thick, like they're striped molasses
Star, on the rise, in the eyes of the masses
Black is the color of my true love's hair
Star's are bright, shining, hot balls of air

Black like my baby girl's stare
Black like the veil that the muslimina wear
Black like the planet that they fear, why they scared?
Black like the slave ship that later brought us here
Black like the cheeks that are roadways for tears
that leave black faces well traveled with years
Black like assassin crosshairs

After a few minutes of writing, Greatness informs Truth, "I got some lines I'm gonna need you to help me out on." Truth nods. He's become fidgety: he plays with his pen, yawns, stares off into the distance, has a drink.

Deep on the front lines, and blacks is all there
Black like the perception of who, on welfare
Black like faces at the bottom of the well
I've been there before
To bring the light and heat it up like "la cocina"
Make what I imagine happen, or maybe I'm just a dreamer
I love rockin' tracks like John Coltrane love Naema

Like the student love the teacher
Like the prophet love Khadeja
Like I love my baby features
Like the creator love all creatures

Who acknowledge truth and peace seekers
We on point like heat seekers
Targettin' the black marketing strategists
Run up on 'em with the heaters
Everybody followin' with no leaders
Feelin' like we killin' ourselves

because I know they can't defeat us
It don't stop til' we complete this, keep this fly
There's so much to life when you just stay Black and die

Blacker than the nighttime sky of Bed-Stuy in July
Blacker than the seed in the blackberry pie
Blacker than the middle of my eye
Black like feh-lah man cry
Some man wan ask "Who am I?"
I simply reply, "The U.N.I.V.E.R.S.A.L. Magnetic"
Work to respect the angelic, climb the mountaintop
and tell it 'til the valley's enveloped
You're full of big chat but you nah know me
I'm dark like the side of the moon you don't see
when the moon shine newly

You know who else is a Black Star? (Who?) Me
You know who else is a Black Star? (Who?) Me
You know who else is a Black Star, who we? (And we)
be shinin' and shinin', when we rhymin' and rhymin'
We be shinin' and shinin', when we rhymin' and rhymin'
Now everybody hop on the one, the sounds of the two
It's the third eye vision, five side dimension
The 8th Light, is gonna shine bright tonight
It's the third eye vision, five side dimension

"This is going to be so high energy, ain't it?"

"It's going to be so hard to remember." Greatness shakes his head. He is pained. "Man, I swear. I hope there's no such thing as a limited time constraint over in Europe."

Now black people unite, and let's ALL GET DOWN
Now everybody hop on the one, the sounds of the two
It's the third eye vision, five side dimension
The 8th Light, is gonna shine bright tonight
Everybody hop on the one, the sounds of the two
It's the third eye vision, five side dimension

"Wait a minute," Greatness says. "Don't we need fucking passports to go over there?"

"We're working on that."
"How much does a passport cost anyway?"
"I don't know. I've got mine."
"Hmm?"
"I've got mine, I don't know."
"Well—"
"Shut the fuck up."
"Thank you Mr. I-got-one-but-can't-help-nobody-else."
"I think it depends."

There is a long silence. Truth plays with his papers, watches Greatness write. He lies down with his head on his notebook—a familiar pose—stretches the fingers of his left hand, and folds his arms across his chest.

"Presidents to represent me"
Get money!"
"I'm out for presidents to represent me"
"Get money!"
"I'm out for presidents to represent me"
"Get money!"
"I'm out for dead fuckin' presidents to represent me (Whose...)"
Rock ... on, Roc-A-Fella y'all
The saga continues

Ahh, who wanna bet us that we don't touch leathers
Stack cheddars forever, live treacherous all the et ceteras
To the death of us, me and my confidantes, we shine
You feel the ambiance, y'all niggas just rhyme
By the ounce dough accumulates like snow
We don't just shine, we illuminate the whole show; you feel me?
Factions from the other side would love to kill me
Spill three quarts of my blood into the street, let alone the heat
Fuck 'em, we hate a nigga lovin' this life
In all possible ways, know the Feds is buggin' my life
Hospital days, reflectin' when my man laid up
On the Uptown high block he got his side sprayed up
I saw his life slippin', this is a minor set back
Yo, still in all we livin', just dream about the get back
That made him smile though his eyes said, "Pray for me"
I'll do you one better and slay these niggas faithfully

Murder is a tough thing to digest, it's a slow process
and I ain't got nothin' but time
I had near brushes, not to mention three shots
close range, never touched me, divine intervention
Can't stop I, from drinkin' Mai-Tai's, with Ty Ty
Down in Nevada, ha ha, Poppa, word life
I dabbled in crazy weight without rap, I was crazy straight
Partner, I'm still spendin' money from eighty-eight... what?
Geyeah, know what? I'll make..
you and your wack mans fold like bad hands
Roll like Monopoly, advance you copy me
like white crystals, I gross the most
at the end of the fiscal year than these niggas can wish to
The dead presidential, candidate
with the sprinkles and the presidential, ice that'll offend you
In due time when crime flees my mind
All sneak thieves and playa haters can shine
But until then I keep the trillion cut diamonds shinin' brilliant
I'll tell you half the story, the rest you fill it in
Long as the villain win
I spend Japan yen, attend major events
Catch me in the joints, convinced my iguanas is bitin'
J-A-Y hyphen, controllin', manipulatin'
I got a good life man, pounds and pence
Nuff dollars make sense, while you ride the bench
Catch me swinging for the fence
Dead Presidents, ya know

Uh-huh, yeah, uh-huh, so be it
The Soviet, The Unified Steady Flow
You already know, you light I'm heavy roll, heavy dough
Mic macheted your flow, your paper falls slow
like confetti, mines a steady grow, bet he glow
Pay five dead it from blow, better believe I have
eleven sixty to show, my doe flip like Tae-Kwon
Jay-Z The Icon, baby, you like Dom, maybe this Cristal's
to change your life huh, roll with the winners
Heavy spenders like hit records: Roc-A-Fella
Don't get it corrected this shit is perfected
from chips to chicks just strip in a Lexus

Make it without your gun, we takin' everything you brung
We cake and you niggas is fake and we gettin' it done
Crime Family, well connected Jay-Z
And you fake thugs is Unplugged like MTV
I empty three, take your treasure, my pleasure
Dead presidentials, politics as usual
Bla-ouw!
Dead fuckin' presidents to represent me (Whose...)

The computer screen behind them goes black. He covers his eyes with his right hand. He scratches his beard. He bites his nails. He cracks his wrist.

"Tag."

"Hit me."

"Your last line?"

"And after Nard hit him with the strike of magic, then poof, just like that, Jeremy was gone."

"Me and poetry had a talk the other day.

"Yes, poetry is a woman, and sometimes a woman has to kill herself to survive.

"Poetry was a life force, a life force that promised that from this day forward, she was feeding herself daily. She reveled in her newfound independence.

"Poetry had a life, and now I'm ready to get my own.

"Poetry had to be elsewhere, but despite my hardships, I held my head high. I'd learned that bad things happened to good people.

"My life was bad; my heart was good. But I'm gonna be ugly today, and I'm gonna be ugly tomorrow: might as well make the best of what God gave me, right?"

They say this is the place stars are born
They say this is the place legends are made
They say this is the place where angels come again,
They say that this is the place where it all can happen for you

Greatness stands up. "And that's all I got." He walks away.

REFERENCES

Carter, Quentin. *Stained Cotton.* New York: Triple Crown Publications, 2008.
CASH. *TRUST NO MAN!* Bloomington: AuthorHouse, 2005.
Covington, Michael. *Chances.* Minneapolis: Triple Crown Publications, 2007.
Ervin, Keisha. *Chyna Black.* Minneapolis: Triple Crown Publications, 2004.
JaQuavis, Ashley. *The Cartel.* Urban, 2008.
King, Deja. *Bitch.* Minneapolis: Triple Crown Publications, 2006.
King, Deja. *Bitch Reloaded.* Minneapolis: Triple Crown Publications, 2007.
King, Deja. *The Bitch is Back.* New York: Triple Crown Publications, 2008.
K'wan. *Gutter.* New York: St. Martin's Griffin, 2008.
Lennox, Lisa. *Crack Head.* Minneapolis: Triple Crown Publications, 2005.
Morrison, Mary B. *Unconditionally Single.* Dafina, 2009.
Sanders, Mike. *Thirsty.* Wahida Clark Presents, 2009.
Santiago, Nisa. *Cartier Cartel.* Melodrama, 2009.
Stringer, Vicki M. *The Reason Why: A Novel.* New York: Atria, 2009.
Styles, Toy. *Black and ugly.* Columbus, Ohio: Triple Crown Publications, 2006.
Swinson, Kiki. *I'm Still Wifey.* New York: Dafina, 2009.
Swinson, Kiki. *Notorious.* New York: Dafina, 2009.
Swinson, Kiki. *Playing Dirty.* Dafina, 2009.
Swinson, Kiki. *Still Wifey Material.* Melodrama, 2008.
Turner, Nikki. *Ghetto Superstar.* New York: One World/Ballantine, 2009.
White, Cynthia. *Queen.* Minneapolis: Triple Crown Publications, 2007.
Woods, Teri. *Alibi.* Grand Central, 2009.

TRACK LIST

GZA, "Liquid Swords" from *Liquid Swords* (1995)
Nas, "Memory Lane" from *Illmatic* (1994)
Wu-Tang Clan, "Protect Ya Neck" from *Enter the Wu-Tang* (1993)
Rakim, "When I B On Tha Mic" from *Master* (1999)
Nas, "2nd Childhood" from *Stillmatic* (2001)
Black Star, "Astronomy (8th Light)" from *Mos Def & Talib Kweli Are Black Star* (2002)
Jay-Z, "Dead Presidents II" from *Reasonable Doubt* (1995)
Eric B. and Rakim, "Don't Sweat the Technique" from *Don't Sweat the Technique* (1992)
Tupac, "Do For Love" from *R U Still Down? Remember Me)* (1997)
Nas, "The World is Yours" from *Illmatic* (1994)
Q-Tip, "We Fight We Love (Remix)" from *The Renaissance* (2009)
Q-Tip, "Blue Girl" from *Kamaal The Abstract* (2009)
Little Brother, "Step It Up" from *Getback* (2007)
Outkast, "Aquemini" from *Aquemini* (1998)
Lupe Fiasco, "Steady Mobbin'" from *Overlooked: Vol. 1* (2008)
Lupe Fiasco, "Paris Tokyo" from *Lupe Fiasco's The Cool* (2007)
Rakim, "It's Been a Long Time" from *The 19th Letter* (1997)
Little Brother, "Lovin' It" from *The Minstral Show* (2005)
Jay-Z, "NYMP" from *Vol. 3: The Life and Times of S. Carter* (1999)
Raekwon, "Ice Cream" from *Only Built 4 Cuban Linx* (1995)
Talib Kweli and Jean Grae, "New York Shit" from *Hip Hop Docktrine: The Official Boondocks Mixtape* (2006)
Common, "Break My Heart" from *Finding Forever* (2007)
Jay-Z, "Can I Live" from *Reasonable Doubt* (1996)
Talib Kweli, "Country Cousins" from *Eardrum* (2007)
Outkast, "Two Dope Boyz (In A Cadillac)" from *ATLiens* (1996)
Outkast, "SpottieOttieDopaliscious" from *Aquemini* (1998)
Little Brother, "After the Party" from *Getback* (2007)
Outkast, "Gasoline Dreams" from *Stankonia* (2000)
Tupac, "Pain" from *Above the Rim: The Soundtrack* (2004)
Notorious BIG, "Sky's The Limit" from *Life After Death* (1997)

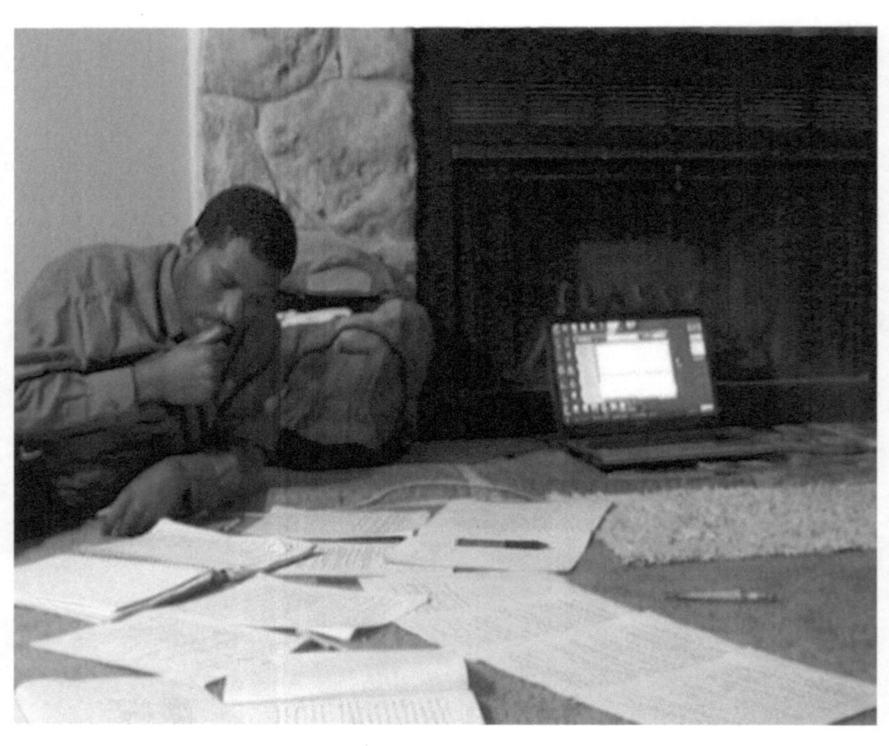

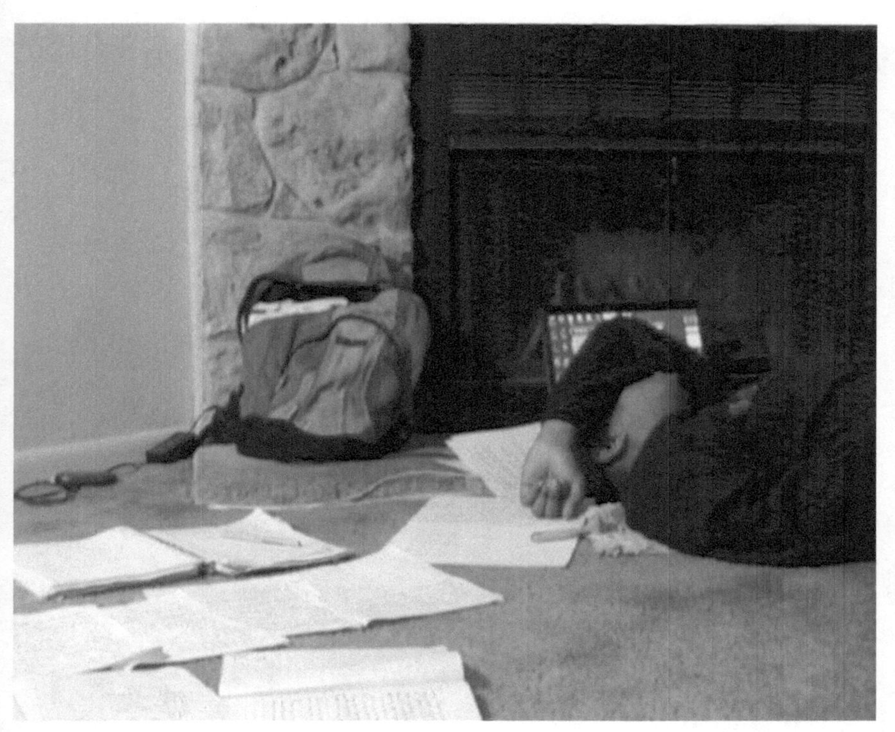

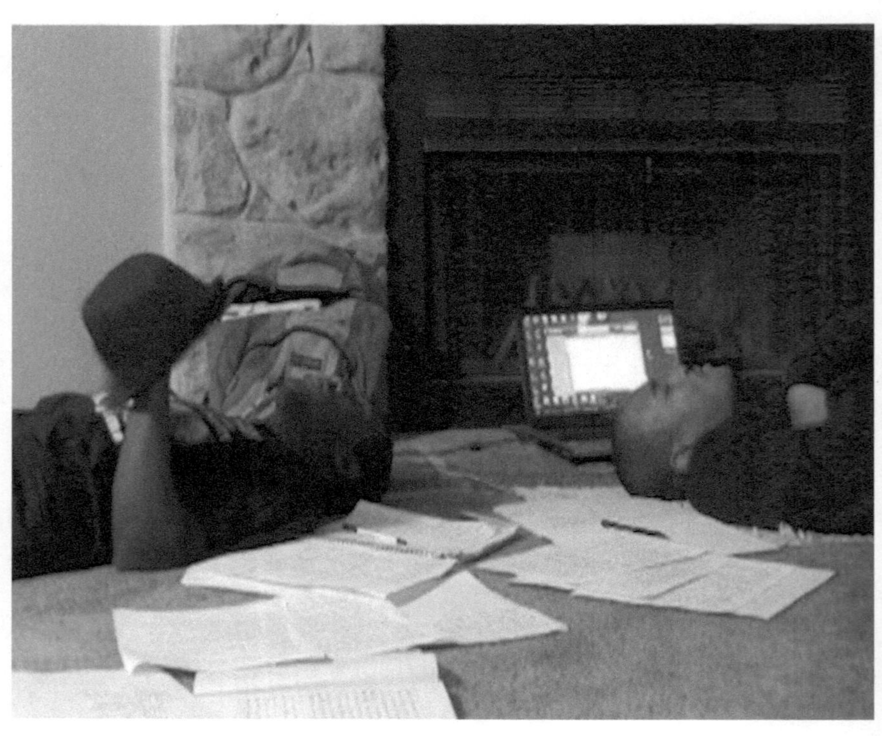

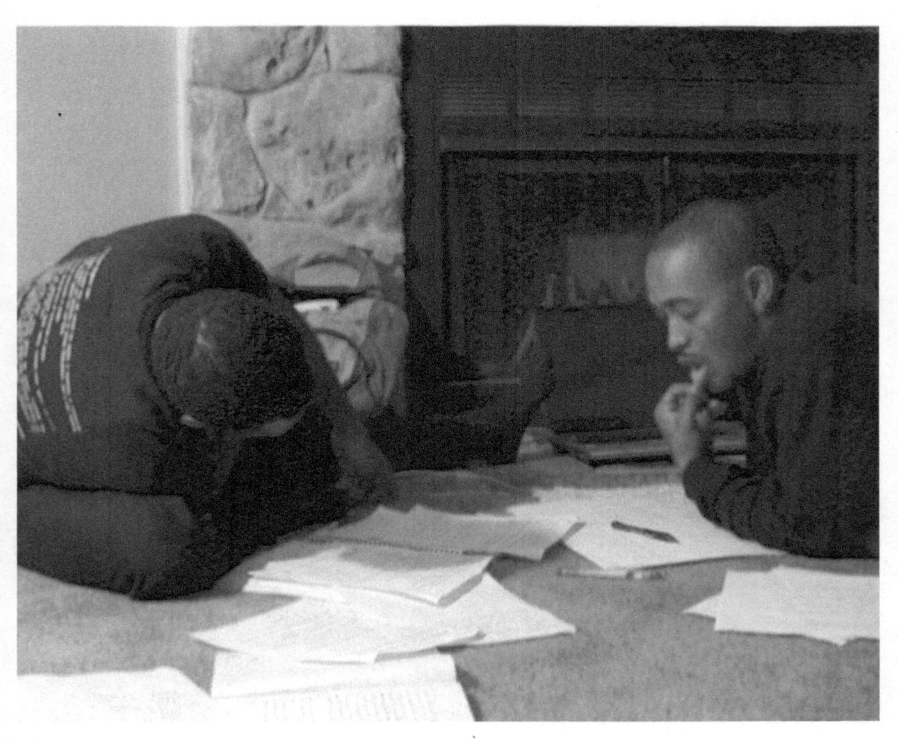

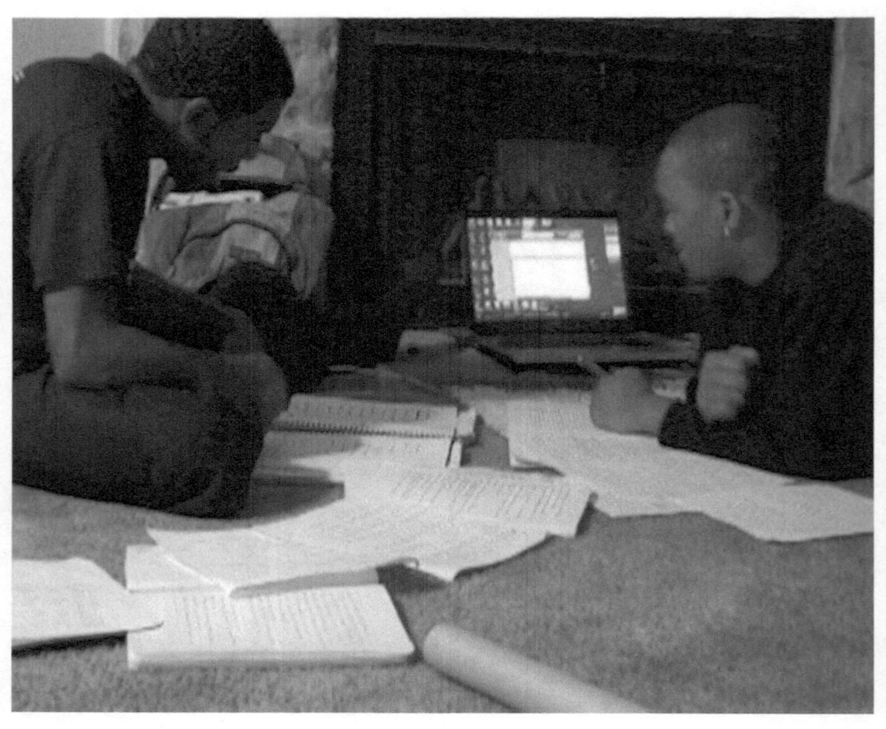

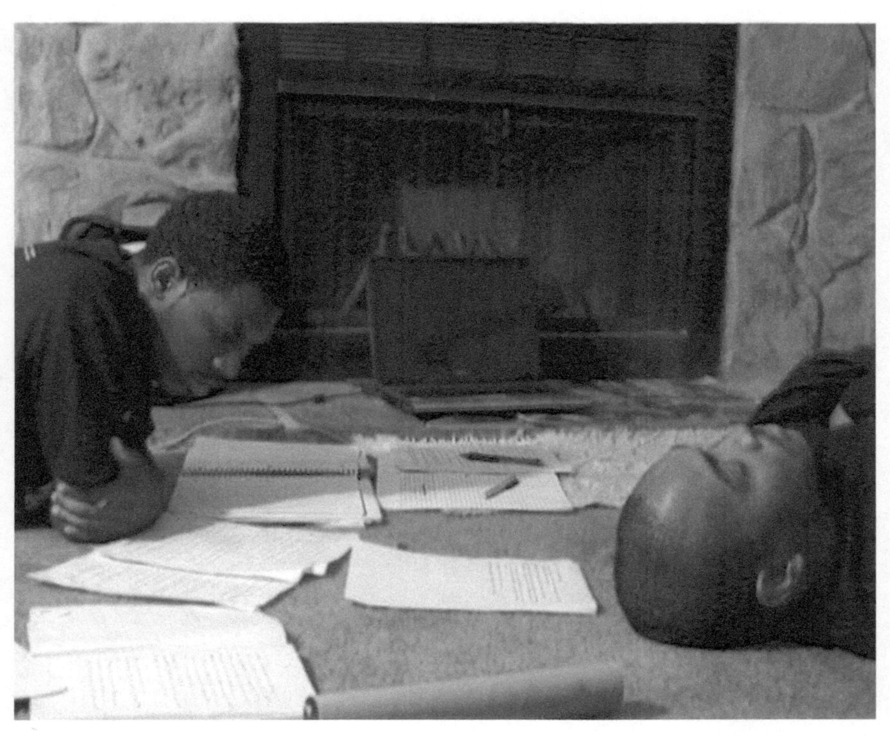

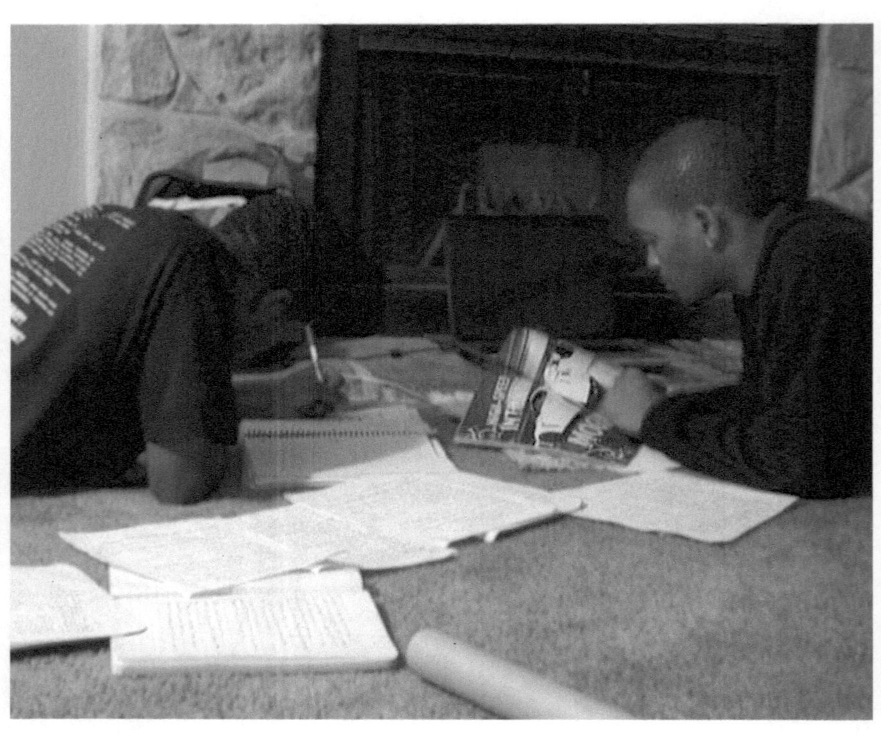

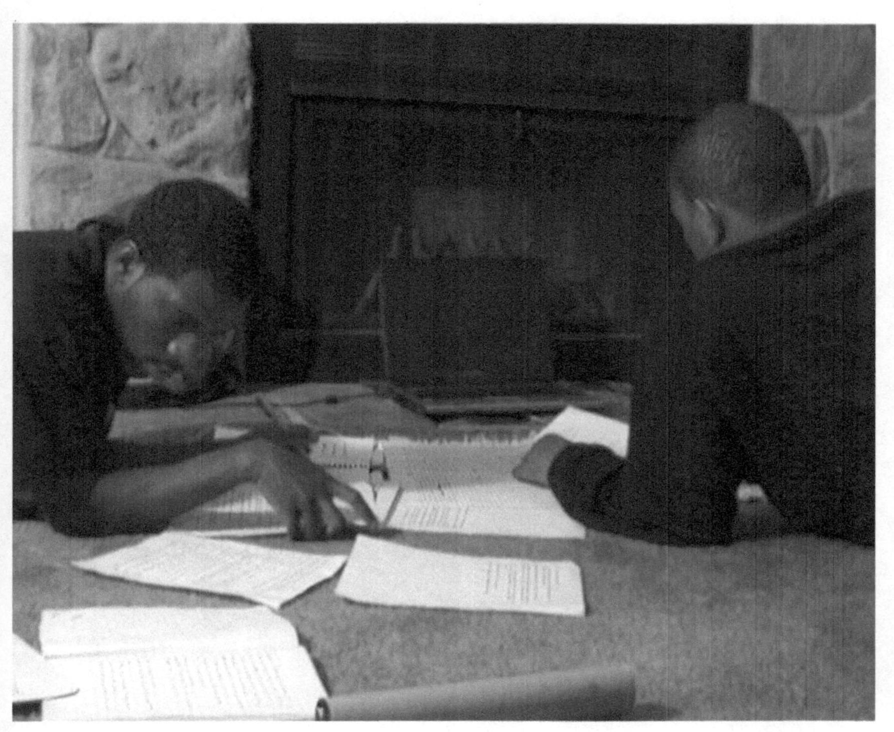

INVISIBLE INK:
THIRD PERSON AUTOBIOGRAPHY

Many say a dream,
Is a premonition,
Of what the future,
Holds,

how was it supposed to go?

Better yet,
What happened to the plan?

You can plan for success
But you can't determine
How you're going to get there,

How do you describe something
When actions speak louder than words?

Through a series of language
That uses signs,
A quote you can't listen to
Because the message is in
Smoke signals

She is gonna kill us,
It's not our fault

We can't blame others,
Because fault lies with the
Person responsible for the task,

I will not be defeated,
Or at least we won't.....

Ladies and Gentlemen,
Boys and girls,
Mammals,
Sea creatures,
Spiritual anomalies,

Allow us to present to you,
Absolutely … … … … … … … …

An- (Wait wait we're gonna let you finish, but STEFFANI JEMISON IS ONE OF THE MOST CREATIVE MINDS OF ALL TIME !!!!)

But that's not enough
Cuz no words are needed,

But to put it simply,
She's a calculated queen,
From which everything was,
Thought out, sketched, then Handmade,

We truly understand the biography,
Of a person by the view-
Point they have given to others,

Not the standard,
But the exception,

No better yet,
The achiever by means,
Of pushing the limits,
And expanding upon new horizons,
(gasp)

Flashback,
Cuz facts are nothing but life's suggestions,
Opinions are nothing more than the choices
We make,

Everything happens,
For a reason,
And your existence,
On this speck in,
The Universe,
Is, well,

Gravitating,

So much so that it's hard,
To explain ourselves,
To you,

Because you put faith
In your eyes,
Listened with your ears,

But you'll never understand
If you don't open your mind,
SEE WHAT WE MEAN!

But we understand
That if we put faith in our ears
And listened with our eyes,

That the communication between us
Would help open our minds,
To the fact that
our goal is to
Help you achieve yours

We are the bristles,
Before and after,
The brush stroke
That you can assist you with,
plowing fields of purpose
And planting seeds
Of wisdom, that grow a
New soul,
To do away with the old,

So with that being said,
Forgive us for our first mistake,

Since November,
Until now,
No since,
2 poets,
On 4212,
In a café,

We have been,
Destined for....
Much more....

Important than a motive is
A motivator, with a motor,
That's what passion does
For you, that's what should be used,
It's a finishing tool,

You are the company that you keep,
And the compay you keep
Speaks volumes about you,

If you have to question a true artist
about their true aspirations
very rarely would you consult with anything,
outside of the paint, on their canvas,
but when we talk to a flower,
He would tell us that:
"art in general is something for me that is an ongoing conversation.
In fact it is a conversation that has been deepened by meeting her—
since her, and because of her"

SO … … …
Ladie and Gentlemen,
Boys and girls,
Mammals,
Sea creatures,
Spiritual anomalies,
Allow us to present to you,
Absolutely … … … … … … … …
Exactly…..
What you thought she was.

But even after all the greetings,
which were transparent from the start,
her critiques,
who watch her closely,
immediately resumed
what they were
doing before she walked up.

A GLASS HALF EMPTY

Day and night people search for answers
Looking for clues
To the one thing they are obligated to
as far as lifetime demands

Be it a responsibility
An unsought circumstance
Or whether it's becoming a part of something
Bigger than themselves

The answer must manifest
When the answer is encrypted
The decoder lies within the next few
Big decisions to take on current
Or following chapters of their life

The best thing as far as
Predicting your next move
Is not thinking too hard about it
At one time,

Take a breather
Re-approach

Refine your search
And re-adjust your television set
If necessary....

Black lights are the only thing

that are supposed to be capable
of writing on these pages,

these pages were welcomed to
thoughts and magic markers
but not ink,

insult would be the proper name
referring to such a title of such
a book that was supposed to have
been outstandingly written by
a selected group
of people

it didn't have to be that
difficult and for the most part it wasn't,

the only part that was supposed to be different
was the author's ink is not
to be seen.....

We have failed miserably.....
Or have we.......?

Inspiration comes,
From the heart,
Which pushes the mind,
To act,

Since we have met Steffani,
This ink which flows,
Was inspired by,
Her mind,
And Written by,
Our hearts,

Thank You,
For keeping us active,

Truth and Greatness would like to thank Quincy Flowers.

Steffani would like to thank Truth and Greatness—for being such generous collaborators—as well as Hannah Ireland, Adebukola Bodunrin, and Quincy Flowers—for being such generous readers. Her work on Truth and Greatness is inspired by and dedicated to her brother, Philip.

ISBN: 978-0-9833815-5-6

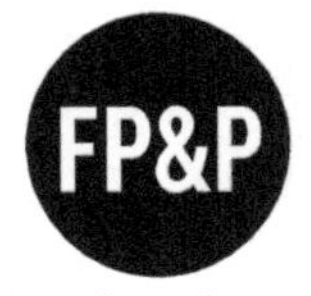

future plan and program

Future Plan and Program
http://futureplanandprogram.com

Please direct inquiries to:
thefuture@futureplanandprogram.com

Series editor: Steffani Jemison
Series designer: Sebastian Civarolo

Future Plan and Program was incubated in 2010-2011 by Project Row Houses.

Acknowledgements: Danielle Burns, Justin Cavin, Aisen Chacin, Ashley Clemmer-Hoffman, Cheryl Flores, Quincy Flowers, Hannah Ireland, Philip Jemison, Steven Jemison, Rick Lowe, Jasmine Jamillah Mahmoud, Phyllis McCallum, Solkem N'Gangbet, Michael Peranteau, Nikki Pressley, Linda Shearer, Martine Syms, Michael Kahlil Taylor, and Julie Thomson.

Future Plan and Program was generously funded in part by the following individuals: Kerry Inman & Denby Auble, John Roberson & John Blackmon, Danielle Antoinette Burns, Justin Cavin, Jereann Chaney, Melody Clark, Ashley Clemmer Hoffman & Brendan Hoffman, Phyllis L. McCallum and Steven Jemison, Joey Romano & Nicole Laurent, Victoria Thomas McGhee, Scott Sawyer & Michael Peranteau, Gregory & Diane Schultz, Leigh & Reggie Smith, and Rebecca Trahan. Special thanks to Jill Whitten & Robert Proctor.

Funding for Steffani Jemison's residency at Project Row Houses was provided by: The National Endowment for the Arts, the City of Houston through the Houston Arts Alliance, Houston Endowment Inc., The Brown Foundation, The Kresge Foundation, The Andy Warhol Foundation for the Visual Arts, and the Texas Commission on the Arts. Steffani Jemison's residency was part of a collaboration with the Core Program at the Glassell School of Art of the Museum of Fine Arts Houston.

www.ingramcontent.com/pod-product-compliance
Lightning Source LLC
LaVergne TN
LVHW091632100826
845152LV00001B/5

* 9 7 8 0 9 8 3 3 8 1 5 5 6 *